W9-BOA-943

DUSTIN PEDROIA

Tammy Gagne

Mitchell Lane
PUBLISHERS

P.O. Box 196
Hockessin, Delaware 19707
Visit us on the web: www.mitchelllane.com
Comments? Email us: mitchelllane@mitchelllane.com

Mitchell Lane
PUBLISHERS

Printing   1   2   3   4   5   6   7   8   9

A Robbie Reader Biography

Abigail Breslin
Adrian Peterson
Albert Einstein
Albert Pujols
Aly and AJ
Andrew Luck
AnnaSophia Robb
Ashley Tisdale
Brenda Song
Brittany Murphy
Buster Posey
Charles Schulz
Chris Johnson
Clayton Kershaw
Cliff Lee
Colin Kaepernick
Dale Earnhardt Jr.
Darius Rucker
David Archuleta

Demi Lovato
Donovan McNabb
Drake Bell & Josh Peck
Dr. Seuss
Dustin Pedroia
Dwayne "The Rock" Johnson
Dwyane Wade
Dylan & Cole Sprouse
Emily Osment
Hilary Duff
Jamie Lynn Spears
Jennette McCurdy
Jesse McCartney
Jimmie Johnson
Joe Flacco
Jonas Brothers
Keke Palmer
Larry Fitzgerald

LeBron James
Mia Hamm
Miguel Cabrera
Miley Cyrus
Miranda Cosgrove
Philo Farnsworth
Raven-Symoné
Robert Griffin III
Roy Halladay
Shaquille O'Neal
Story of Harley-Davidson
Sue Bird
Syd Hoff
Tiki Barber
Tim Lincecum
Tom Brady
Tony Hawk
Troy Polamalu
Victor Cruz
Victoria Justice

Library of Congress Cataloging-in-Publication Data
Gagne, Tammy.
 Dustin Pedroia / by Tammy Gagne.
    pages cm. — (A Robbie reader)
 Includes bibliographical references and index.
 ISBN 978-1-61228-638-9 (library bound)
 1. Pedroia, Dustin. 2. Baseball players—United States—Biography. I. Title.
 GV865.P43G34 2015
 796.357092—dc23
 [B]
                                                                                    2014008323
 eBook ISBN: 9781612286631

ABOUT THE AUTHOR: Tammy Gagne is the author of numerous books for adults and children, including Colin Kaepernick, Darius Rucker, and Hope Solo for Mitchell Lane Publishers. She resides in northern New England with her husband and son. One of her favorite pastimes is visiting schools to speak to kids about the writing process.

PUBLISHER'S NOTE: The following story has been thoroughly researched and to the best of our knowledge represents a true story. While every possible effort has been made to ensure accuracy, the publisher will not assume liability for damages caused by inaccuracies in the data, and makes no warranty on the accuracy of the information contained herein. This story has not been authorized or endorsed by Dustin Pedroia.

TABLE OF CONTENTS

Words in bold type can be found in the glossary.

Dustin Pedroia's mind has long been in the game by the time the umpire yells, "Play ball!" The Boston Red Sox second baseman is seen here shifting his position for a bunt in a 2014 game between the Sox and the Detroit Tigers. Boston would win with a final score of 5 to 3.

The Early Bird . . .

Many hardcore baseball fans show up hours before a game. So does one of the game's most dedicated players. Long before the crowds start gathering outside Fenway Park in Boston, Massachusetts, Dustin Pedroia is hard at work. It isn't a new habit for the Red Sox second baseman. He's done it since he played Little League in his home state of California. Back then he would arrive two hours early. Now it's closer to six hours.

"It's basically a comfortable spot for me. It's a place where I've been all my life," he explained to the *Boston Globe* in 2011. "I think it's a thing that kind of calms me down before a game."

It's not unusual for athletes to have obsessive habits. Many always take the same route to the ballpark or wear a certain piece of jewelry during every game. Dustin insists that it's not about **superstition** for him. "I don't need to do all the stuff I do. It's just that I like it."

It seems to work for him–and his team. Since being drafted by the Red Sox in 2004, Dustin has done some impressive

Dustin's enthusiasm is obvious in the way he plays the game. Here, he tries to complete a double play despite a hard slide by Justin Upton of the Atlanta Braves during a 2014 game. Boston would win that game 8 to 6.

It looked like the Oakland Athletics were going to win their game against Boston on June 21, 2014. But Dustin scored on a wild pitch in the eighth inning to tie the score at 1-1. Still, the A's managed to win the game 2 to 1 in the 10th inning.

things. He was American League Rookie of the Year in 2007 as the Red Sox swept the World Series. And that was just for starters.

Dustin holds his 18-month-old son Dylan during a break in the 2010 State Farm Home Run Derby. Dustin wasn't much older than this when his mother coached his first T-ball team. Maybe he will follow in her coaching footsteps with his children.

CHAPTER TWO

The Drive to Succeed

Dustin Luis Pedroia came into the world on August 17, 1983 in Woodland, California. His parents, Guy and Debbie, owned a tire shop in the small town just north of Sacramento. As a boy, Dustin worked in the family business. Sweeping the warehouse floor was his job.

Dustin isn't the first athlete in the Pedroia household. His mother played tennis in college. She coached her son when he played T-Ball as a toddler. Guy thinks that Dustin got his intense drive for sports from Debbie. "She was tough," he told *Boston Magazine*. "She couldn't win by a big enough **margin** to make her happy."

Dustin's older brother Brett also played baseball. A talented catcher, he was forced to quit the game at the college level when he broke his ankle.

Dustin seemed to excel at every sport. He played basketball and football in addition to baseball.

Dustin was always one of the best players on the baseball field. But he was also one of the smallest. Today he stands 5 feet, 8 inches tall and weighs 170 pounds. In high school, he was even smaller—just five-foot-three and 140 pounds. Rob Bruno was the coach of a travel team that often played against Dustin. He told *Boston Magazine*, "He was a 15-year-old who looked like a 13-year-old playing like an 18-year-old."

"I'm not the biggest guy in the world," Dustin acknowledged in Canada's *National Post*. "I don't have that many tools. If I'm walking down the street, you obviously wouldn't think I'm a baseball player. I think that's the biggest thing that [drives] me to be a good player. I've had to deal with it my

whole life. That's just been **instilled** in my mind, that I have to overcome everything to prove people wrong. So far, I've done that."

Red Sox general manager Theo Epstein agrees. He told *Boston Magazine*, "His size is part of who he is. His whole life people have been reacting to him, initially, in a certain manner, and his whole life he's been channeling that and turning it around and laughing as he steps right over them."

Dustin's hard work and determination on the field are unsurpassed. He gives every practice and game his absolute best. Others might see things like his smaller size as limitations. But to Dustin his weaknesses only drive him to succeed all the more.

Dustin has never let his smaller stature hold him back. Whether playing for Arizona State University (as shown here) or the Boston Red Sox, he has always given the game his all. And it has paid off.

CHAPTER THREE

Putting His Team First

Dustin was the star of the Woodland High School baseball team. As a senior, he had a batting average of .455. But college scouts didn't seem to notice him. All that changed when he played in a state-wide tournament called the Area Code Games. He did so well in the competition that Arizona State University offered him a **scholarship**.

Dustin continued to excel as a hitter and shortstop for the Sun Devils. He took his responsibilities as a player very seriously. In his entire time at Arizona State, he never missed a single game. His freshman year, he helped his team win 37 games. They came in third in the NCAA Regionals. But something he did after his freshman year showed just how deep his sportsmanship ran.

College athletes know that their performance usually makes or breaks their chances of making it at the professional level. For this reason, many try to take the spotlight as much as possible. But Dustin knew that the best way to make his own baseball dreams come true was by helping his team to succeed. He believed a junior college pitcher named Ben Thurmond could contribute to that success.

Dustin knew that Ben needed a scholarship to attend Arizona State. But none were available when he was ready to transfer. Dustin explained to the *Boston Globe*, "I told the coaches, 'If we can get this guy, he can have my scholarship.' I wanted to win the [College] World Series. I asked my parents and they said OK."

Despite Dustin's **sacrifice**, the Sun Devils didn't get a chance to win the World Series. They lost to California State Fullerton

Though he now plays second base, Dustin was a shortstop at Arizona State. Here he rifles a throw to first base after scooping up a ground ball.

in the regionals. Still, Dustin had no regrets. He told the *Boston Globe*, "It was the right thing to do. Ben was a great teammate and a great friend."

It seemed clear that Dustin would go far in baseball. Before reaching the Major League, though, he had to put in his time on minor-league teams. Here he fields a grounder while playing for the Portland (Maine) Sea Dogs. As a Sea Dog, he made the switch from shortstop to second base.

Sometimes Nice Guys Finish First

Dustin was making a name for himself at Arizona State. After his junior year in 2004, he was named a finalist for the Golden Spikes Award. This honor is given to the country's top amateur player. At the same time, Boston chose Dustin in the second round of the Major League Baseball Draft. They offered him a signing bonus of $575,000 to become part of *their* team.

He did well that summer in the lower levels of the minor leagues, then began the 2005 season with the Portland (Maine) Sea Dogs. Instead of playing shortstop, he became the team's second baseman. He handled the **transition** like a pro. People were still talking about his size. But it wasn't stopping him from moving up the ranks. Later that season he was promoted to the Pawtucket (Massachusetts) Red Sox. He played for Pawtucket in 2006, and was called up to play for Boston at the end of the season. Shortly after Dustin received the big news, he told the *Boston Globe*, "They were kind of like, 'Get packed up and head down the road.' It's been a hectic last 12 hours. It's kind of a shock to me, too. They just told me, 'You're going up. You'll play there. Have fun.' Each step you go up it's more and more fun."

Even though Dustin didn't hit very well, he still had fun. More important, he felt like he belonged at the Major League level.

Dustin's performance with Boston in the 2007 season overcame all the discussion about his **stature**. He had a batting average of .317. He hit 39 doubles and 8 home runs, and had 50 RBIs. These impressive numbers earned him the American League Rookie of the Year award.

Dustin racked up a lot of experience in a short amount of time in the minors. He is seen here during a 2006 International League game in Rochester, New York as a member of the Pawtucket (Massachusetts) Red Sox. They are also known as the PawSox, as the front of his uniform shows.

Dustin and his Red Sox teammates know how to work together. Here, outfielder Coco Crisp jumps out of the way to allow Dustin to field the ball in a 2007 game against the New York Yankees. The Sox would win that game with a final score of 10 to 1.

Dustin is confident whether he is at bat or on the field. When he steps up to the plate, the opposing team knows that he is as accomplished at hitting as he is at manning second base. Here he is seen taking a pitch during a game between the Boston Red Sox and the Baltimore Orioles.

Dustin's hard work continued to pay off in the postseason. His batting average in the American League Championship Series was .354. He scored more runs than any other player as Boston defeated the Cleveland Indians. Batting a respectable .278 in the World Series, Dustin hit a home run and had four RBIs as Boston swept the Colorado Rockies four games to none.

To his fans, Dustin was already the Most Valuable Player in Major League Baseball. But they wanted to make it official. Here, a passionate fan holds up a sign expressing her desire for him to win the celebrated award.

At Home in Boston

Dustin was even better in 2008. His batting average was .326. He led the league in hits, runs scored, and doubles. He hammered 17 home runs, drove in 83 runs, and stole 20 bases. Those numbers earned him the American League's Most Valuable Player (MVP) award, making him only the third player to be Rookie of the Year and MVP in successive seasons. But the Red Sox couldn't make it back to the World Series. The Tampa Bay Rays defeated them in the American League Championship Series.

Boston rewarded Dustin for his hard work and accomplishments with a new contract. It was worth $40.5 million and covered the next six seasons. That would prove to be long enough for another chance at the World Series.

Dustin and his Red Sox teammates made it back to the World Series in 2013. This time they had an extra **incentive** to win. On April 15, two bombs had exploded at the Boston Marathon. Three people were killed, with dozens of others seriously injured. Following the attack, the people of Boston united.

Dustin makes time to sign balls for some of his fans in Florida in 2013. Even though he was hundreds of miles from Boston, he still had many supporters in the stands at Tropicana Field before the Sox's game against the Tampa Bay Rays that day.

Dustin poses with the World Series Trophy in 2013 at Fenway Park in Boston, Massachusetts. His hard work and dedication helped the Red Sox win the Series in 2007. He and the team would do it again in 2013–this time against the St. Louis Cardinals.

When the Sox won the World Series by defeating the St. Louis Cardinals, Dustin told the *Tribune News Service*, "We got together in spring training and everyone cared about each other so much. The stuff that happened in this city, we wanted to do something special. Hopefully we did that."

Dustin has made quite a life for himself in Boston. In 2006 he married his college sweetheart, Kelli. The couple has two sons,

In addition to being a star baseball player, Dustin Pedroia is also a husband and a father. He is seen here with his wife Kelli and their sons, Dylan and Cole during the 2013 All-Star Red Carpet Parade in New York City.

Dylan and Cole. Dustin wrote in his autobiography, *Born to Play: My Life in the Game,* "I love it in Boston and my wife loves it, too. The team treats players' families unbelievably well. They make everything as easy as they can because the only thing they want you to worry about is baseball. You won't find that **philosophy** in many other places."

Of course, he is paid very well for the work he is doing. But Dustin insists that his salary isn't the driving force. "I really don't play for money," he told the *Boston Globe.* "I play because I love the game, and because I want to make an impact. I hope to play for the Red Sox a long time."

The Red Sox agreed with this hope. In July, 2013, they signed Dustin to a 7-year, $100-million contract extension. "I live or die by this team," he told ESPN. It's important to me to be here my entire time."

Almost certainly he will be.

STATISTICS

YEAR	G	AB	R	H	2B	3B	HR	BA	RBI	SB
2006	31	89	5	17	4	0	2	.191	7	0
2007	139	520	86	165	39	1	8	.317	50	7
2008	157	653	118*	213*	54*	2	17	.326	83	20
2009	154	626	115*	185	48	1	15	.296	45	5
2010	75	302	53	87	9	1	12	.288	41	9
2011	159	635	102	195	37	3	21	.307	91	26
2012	141	563	81	163	39	3	15	.290	65	20
2013	160	641	91	193	42	2	9	.301	84	17
2014	109	442	56	124	29	0	5	.281	42	3

2014 Statistics as of August 6, 2014
G = Games; AB = At-bats; R = Runs; H = Hits; 2B = Doubles; 3B = Triples; HR = Home runs; BA = Batting average; RBI = Runs batted in; SB = Stolen bases; * = Led league

CHRONOLOGY

1983	Dustin is born on August 17th.
2002	Dustin begins his baseball career with the Arizona State Sun Devils.
2004	The Boston Red Sox take Dustin in the second round of the Major League Baseball Draft.
2005	Dustin shifts from shortstop to second base as he plays for the Portland Sea Dogs.
2006	Dustin makes his Major League debut on August 22.
2007	Dustin wins American League Rookie of the Year award.
2008	Dustin is named American League's Most Valuable Player.
2010	A major foot injury sidelines Dustin for much of the season.
2011	Dustin's 25-game hitting streak is the longest-ever by a Boston second baseman.
2014	Dustin hits his 100th career home run, a grand slam on May 2 against Oakland.

FIND OUT MORE

Books

Gaspar, Joe. *Dustin Pedroia*. New York: Powerkids Press, 2010.

Pedroia, Dustin. *Born to Play: My Life in the Game*. New York: Gallery Books, 2010.

On the Internet

Ask Dustin Pedroia, Sports Illustrated Kids
http://www.sikids.com/contests/ask-dustin-pedroia

Dustin Pedroia, Boston Red Sox
http://boston.redsox.mlb.com/team/player.jsp?player_id=456030#gameType='R'&sectionType=career&statType=1&season=2014&level='ALL'

Works Consulted

Abraham, Peter. "The art of being Dustin Pedroia." *Boston Globe*, July 14, 2013.

Boland, Erik. "Red Sox have much to celebrate." *Tribune News Service,* October 31, 2013.

Craggs, Tommy. "Dustin Pedroia Comes Out Swinging." *Boston Magazine*, April 2009. http://www.bostonmagazine.com/2009/03/dustin-pedroia/

"Dustin Pedroia," jockbio.com. http://www.jockbio.com/Bios/Pedroia/Pedroia_bio.html

Edes, Gordon. "Dustin Pedroia Not Going Anywhere." ESPN, July 23, 2013. http://espn.go.com/boston/mlb/story/_/id/9503933/dustin-pedroia-contract-extension-keep-where-belongs

———. "Pedroia's success isn't small-town news." *Boston Globe*, June 5, 2007.

FIND OUT MORE

Lott, Jon. "Boston's Pedroia comes up big; Wins AL MVP Award; Diminutive second baseman piles up hardware." *National Post* (Canada), November 19, 2008.

Pedroia, Dustin. *Born to Play: My Life in the Game*. New York: Gallery Books, 2010.

Snow, Chris. "Pedroia on Fast Track." *Boston Globe*, June 23, 2005.

Thompson, Rich. "No keeping Dustin Pedroia down." *Tribune Business News*, August 19, 2013.

GLOSSARY

incentive (in-SEN-tihv)–Something that makes a person want to work hard.

instill (in-STIL)–Gradually establish an idea or a quality in someone's mind.

margin (MAHR-jin)–Boundary area.

philosophy (fih-LOS-uh-fee)–Basic beliefs about the way people should live or act.

sacrifice (SAK-ruh-fise)–Give up something for the sake of someone or something else.

scholarship (SKAHL-uhr-ship)–Money given to a student by a college to help pay for his or her education.

stature (STACH-uhr)–A person's height.

superstition (soo-per-STIH-shuhn)–A belief or practice resulting from ignorance, fear of the unknown, or trust in magic.

transition (tran-ZISH-uhn)–Changing from one state, stage, place, or subject to another.

INDEX